CLASSIC STAINED GLASS VECTOR DESIGNS

CLASSIC STAINED GLASS VECTOR DESIGNS

DOVERPICTURA

DOVER PUBLICATIONS, INC. | Mineola, New York

By Alan Weller.
Designed by Joel Waldrep.

Classic Stained Glass Vector Designs is a new work, first published by Dover Publications, Inc., in 2009.

For permission to use more than ten images, please contact:
Permissions Department
Dover Publications, Inc.
31 East 2nd Street
Mineola, NY 11501
rights@doverpublications.com

The CD-ROM file names correspond to the images in the book. All of the artwork stored on the CD-ROM can be imported directly into a wide range of design and word-processing programs on either Windows or Macintosh platforms. No further installation is necessary.

ISBN 10: 0-486-99024-9
ISBN 13: 978-0-486-99024-8
Manufactured in the United States of America
Dover Publications, Inc., 31 East 2nd Street, Mineola, NY 11501
www.doverpublications.com

GALLERY–PAGES 1, 2, 4, 8 thru 29

Provides you with examples, from basic to complex, of compositions designed using vectors and textures from the accompanying CD. On the right-hand side of each pair of pages is an 'asset panel,' in which you will find a listing of all of the components and colors that were used in the creation of the illustrations.

TUTORIALS–PAGES 30 thru 49

Contains instructional materials pertaining to the examples shown in the Gallery section of this book. Use this section to learn how work with vector images and to create your own compositions in Adobe Illustrator. These tutorials will teach you about basic elements such as shapes, paths, and anchor points, and will give you step-by-step instructions for coloring, reshaping, scaling and patterning.

STAINED GLASS TEXTURES–PAGES 50 and 51

Shows simple, clean renderings of all of the texture glass images that are on the accompanying CD.

VECTORS–PAGES 52 thru 127

Shows simple, clean renderings of all of the vector images that are on the accompanying CD.

042

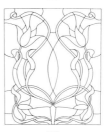

171

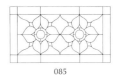

085

Texture 1

Texture 2

Smoke 1

Swirl 2

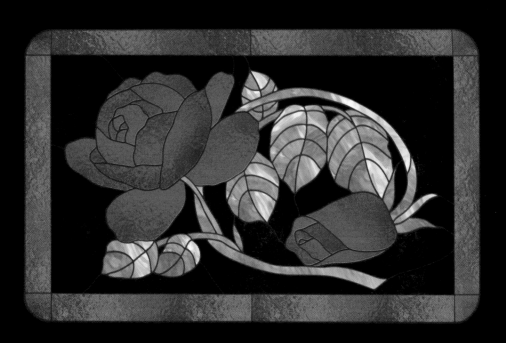

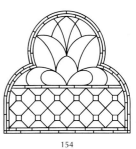

154

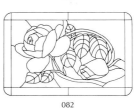

082

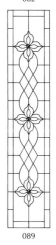

089

Texture 1

Smoke 2

Swirl 1

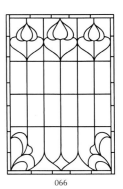

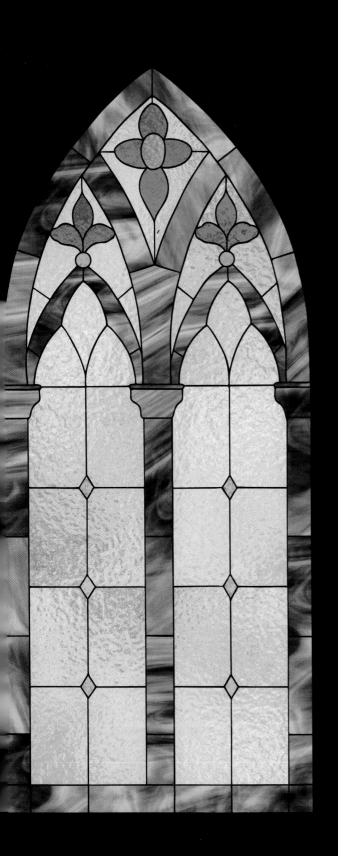

066

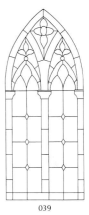

039

Texture 2

Smoke 1

Smoke 2

13

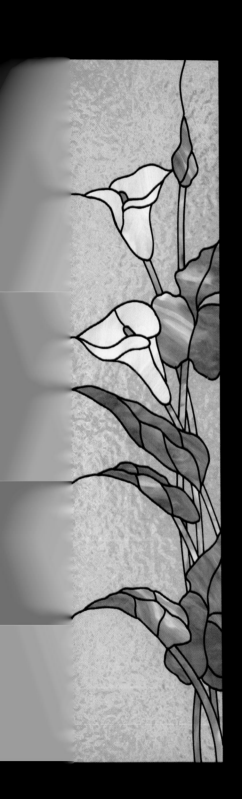

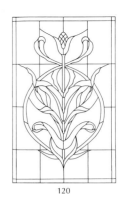

120

030   031

Texture 1

Texture 2

Smoke 1

15

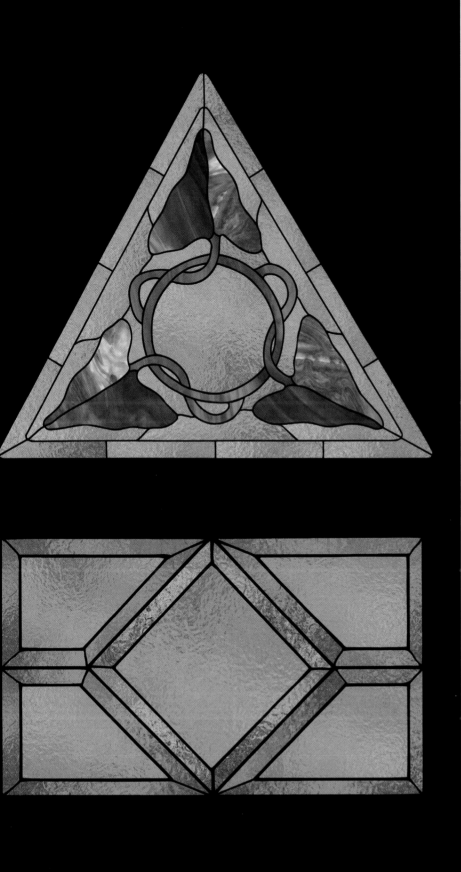

024

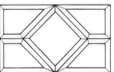

118

127

Texture 1

Texture 2

Smoke 1

Swirl 2

192

032

Texture 1

Smoke 1

Swirl 2

19

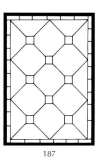

187

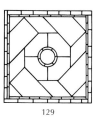

129

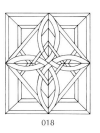

018

Texture 1

Texture 2

Smoke 1

054

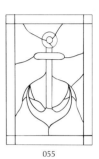

055

Texture 1

Texture 2

Smoke 1

099

116

Smoke 1

Smoke 2

Swirl 1

126

178

Smoke 1

Smoke 2

Swirl 1

Swirl 2

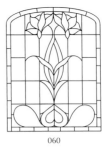

060

058

Texture 1

Texture 2

Smoke 1

Swirl 2

About These Tutorials

The following are basic instructional tutorials for the techniques used to create the illustrations within the Gallery section of this book. These illustrations were created using Adobe Illustrator, and a basic working knowledge of this program is important to mastering these techniques. More in-depth information about this program can be found under the Adobe Illustrator Help tab, or by visiting the Adobe website at www.adobe.com.

These tutorials have been performed using the Macintosh version of Adobe Illustrator CS2. If you have a newer or older version of Illustrator, some variation could occur in how your software displays the tools used in these tutorials. Also, there are minor differences in functionality and nomenclature between the Windows and Macintosh versions of Illustrator. Consult your Illustrator manual or the Help tab if you do not find the Tool, Window, Menu, or Palette described in the tutorial.

Opening Vectors in Illustrator

1. On the top menu bar, go to the drop-down menu File>Open.

2. In the Open Window, locate the Dover CD which is in your computer's CD drive, double click.

3. Double click on the 'Images' folder

4. Double click on the subfolder that contains the image that you wish to open.

5. Double click on the vector file that you wish to open.

Some Basics about Vectors

Unlike bit-mapped images which are composed of pixels, vector graphics use points, lines, and curves to define shapes. Because of this they are 'resolution independent,' and can be reshaped, scaled, or resized without a loss of image quality. Please note that the final quality of your image will be determined by the resolution of your printer, or when viewing on-screen, by the quality of your monitor.

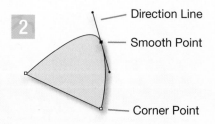

1. A vector 'path' can either be open (like the curved line) or closed (like the circle).

2. Paths are made up of segments that create the entire shape. Each segment is defined by anchor points. Anchor points can be corner points or smooth points; points can be manipulated using direction lines to change the curvature of the segment.

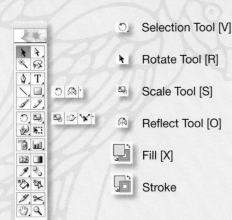

↻   Selection Tool [V]

↖   Rotate Tool [R]

▢   Scale Tool [S]

◈   Reflect Tool [O]

▣   Fill [X]

▣   Stroke

This is a list of the basic tools used in the tutorials. If the Tool bar is not displayed it can be accessed from the top menu bar by going Window>Tools. The Tool bar is extremely handy, and gives quick access to the basic design tools. Some variant tools are hidden from view, and can be accessed by clicking and holding down the mouse over a related tool's icon. Tools with variants have small arrows in the bottom right hand corner of their icon.

To learn more about the Tool bar, search under the Help tab, or in the manual that accompanied your software.

This is a list of the basic Palettes used in the tutorials. Most palettes can be accessed from the top menu bar by going to Window>Palettes.
Please note that in Adobe Illustrator Palettes can also be referred to as Windows.

Swatches Palette

Layers Palette

Gradient Palette

Transform Palette

Align Palette

In addition to Adobe Illustrator and Photoshop, for which we have included instructional material within this book, there are many other software programs that allow you to use and edit vector-based images. Most of these programs are proprietary and must purchased, however, there are several open-source, freeware and shareware programs available for download over the internet. A good resource for information about both commercial and free software can be found at the following link:

http://en.wikipedia.org/wiki/List_of_vector_graphics_editors

There are several basic types of software programs with which vector images can be utilized.
The following is a list of the most popular, by category.

Illustration:

Adobe Illustrator	www.adobe.com/products/illustrator
Corel Draw	www.corel.com
Microsoft Expression Suite	www.microsoft.com/expression

Page layout:

Adobe InDesign	www.adobe.com/products/indesign
Quark XPress	www.quark.com
Scribus	www.scribus.net

Web and web animation:

Adobe Flash	www.adobe.com/products/flash
Adobe Fireworks	www.adobe.com/products/fireworks

Photo editing:

Adobe Photoshop	www.adobe.com/products/photoshop
Paint Shop Pro	www.corel.com

Image editors:

Xara Xtreme	www.xara.com
Inkscape	www.inkscape.org

About Dover Vectors

Most of the vector images contained in this book come from rare, old sources. In creating these vectors we have tried to maintain the unique intrinsic qualities of the original artwork, while imbuing them with all of the utility that the vector file format affords. Generally, the images in this publication are of two types: regular, closed-cell illustrations which can be 'released' into individual, manipulable shapes; and more expressive, "hand-drawn" illustrations. Please note that because of the complex nature of the latter, the best results in working with this type of image require a fast computer with large allocation of RAM. The simplest method for making more RAM available to Adobe Illustrator is to shut down all unnecessary software programs.

The expressive potential of compositions made with vector images is limitless. In addition to print layouts they can be used to create silkscreen stencils, embroidery patterns, or signage designs to be cut in vinyl. They can be combined with bit-mapped images, used as paths along which type can be flowed, or as texture in multilayered compositions. Vectors tend to be relatively small files, and work very well with programs that generate web graphics, such as Adobe Flash and Fireworks. We encourage you to experiment with these images and to be creative!

Scaling an Image in Illustrator

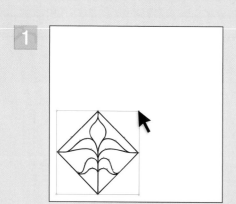

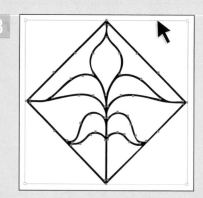

1. Select the image using the Selection Tool found at the top left corner of the tool bar [V]. A box will appear around the image.

2. Grab one of the corners of the box and drag it out diagonally to enlarge it. To reduce the image, drag it in. To scale the image proportionally, hold down the shift key while dragging.

3. Enlarged image.

4. You can also enlarge the image with the Transform Palette. Click the chain icon at the right of the palette to link the width and height together and scale proportionally.

5. To scale proportionally, enter either the desired width or height. To scale non-proportionally, both width and height must be entered.

6. Try the Scale Tool [S] found in the tool bar to achieve similar results.

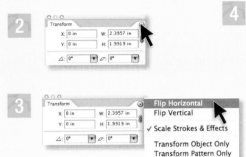

This is also called reflecting the image.

1. Select the image using the Selection Tool found at the top left corner of the tool bar [V].

2. On the top menu bar, go to the drop-down menu Window>Transform to open the Transform Palette. Click on the arrow in the upper right hand corner of the palette.

3. Choose Flip Horizontal

4. The image should be a mirror "reflection" of the original image.

5. This process can also be achieved using the Reflect Tool [O] found in the tool bar.

Rotating an Image in Illustrator

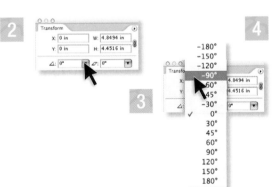

1. Select the image using the Selection Tool found at the top left corner of the tool bar [V].

2. On the top menu bar, go to the drop-down menu Window>Transform to open the Transform Palette. Click on the arrow next to the rotate input field at the lower left of the palette.

3. Select the desired angle from the pop-up list or enter the desired angle directly into the field.

4. The image should rotate.

5. The Rotate Tool [R] found in the tool bar can produce similar results.

Adding Color to Your Palette in Illustrator

At some point you will want to add colors to
your palette. Here is one way to do this.

1. On the top menu bar, go to the drop-down menu
    Windows>Swatches. This will open the Swatches
    Palette window. Select a color swatch. Click the
    Add New Swatch button in the lower right
    corner of the window next to the trashcan.

2. The Swatch Options window should appear. Change the
    color using the sliders at the bottom of the palette.
    You can change the mode using the drop-down
    Color Mode button. The global option will allow you
    to assign a color and change it globally in your
    document. Color type can be either Spot for PMS
    spot colors or Process for CMYK process colors.

3. When you finish creating the color swatch, type in a
    name for it and click the OK button.

4. Figure 4 shows the new orange swatch in the palette.

5. To add additional colors, repeat steps 1, 2, and 3.

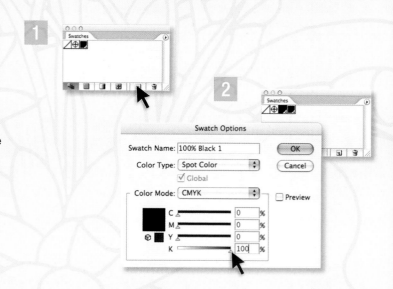

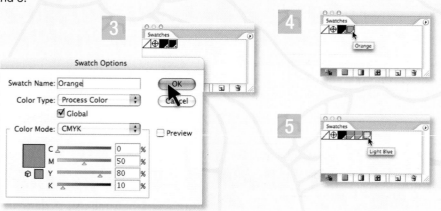

Using A Limited Palette

A limited color palette helps you organize, harmonize,
and set the mood for individual projects. A cool palette
might consist of blues and grays; while a warmer
palette would have more reds and yellows. If you
are designing an image of a sunset, you won't need
cool colors, so why add them to your palette?

Most of the examples shown in this book give the color
palette used for both CMYK and RGB color modes.

	0c	50m	80y	10k
	30c	0m	30y	0k
	30c	0m	10y	0k

	223r	135g	65b
	179r	221g	192b
	174r	223g	228b

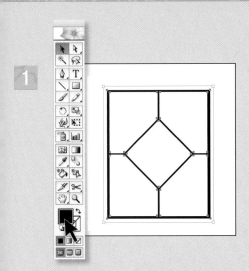

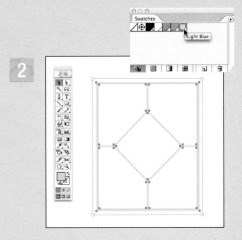

1. Select the image using the Selection Tool found at the top left corner of the tool bar [V].

   Select the fill square from the tool bar [K].

2. Fill the image by clicking on a color from the Swatches Palette Window.

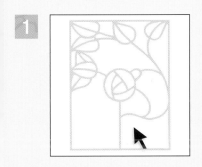

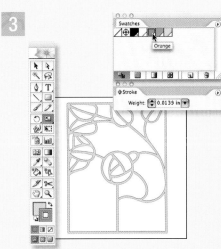

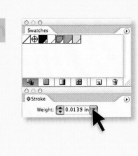

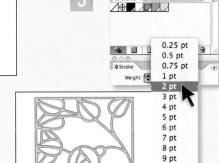

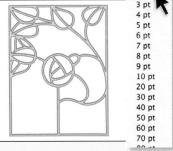

1. Select the image using the Selection Tool found at the top left corner of the tool bar [V].

2. Select the stroke square from the tool bar [X].

3. Stroke the image by clicking on a color from the Swatches Palette window.

4. Change the size of the stroke by clicking on the blue arrow to the immediate right of the stroke input field.

5. Choose the designed stroke weight from the pop-up window or type in the desired weight.

35

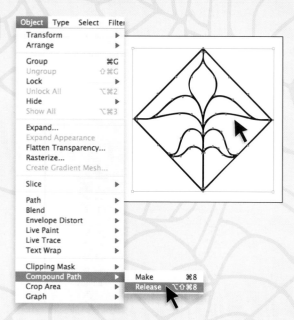

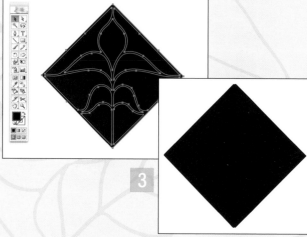

In order to work (color, stroke, drop shadow, etc.)
with the individual cells in a compound path,
you need to release the compound path.

1. Select the image using the Selection Tool
   found at the top left corner of the tool bar [V].

   Go to the drop-down menu Object>Compound
   Path>Release on the top menu bar.

2. Your image should look similar to Figure 2.
   Each individual shape that comprises the
   image is highlighted.

   These shapes are now independent of each other.

3. Deselect the image.

4. Select the image again and fill the top shape
   with a color.

5. With the shape still selected go to the drop-down
   menu Object>Arrange>Send to Back on the
   top menu bar.

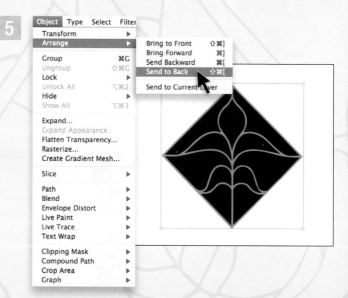

6. The colored shape should now be behind all the other shapes.

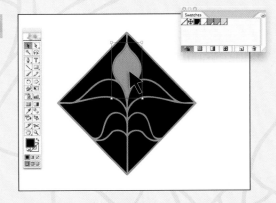

7. Select one of the black shapes remaining and fill with a color.

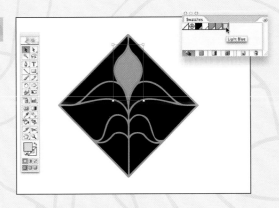

8. Once a new color has been applied to the shape, your image should look similar to Figure 8.

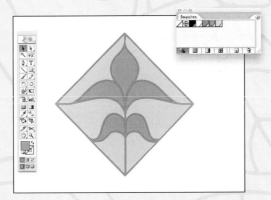

9. Continue selecting the shapes and filling them with color to complete the image.

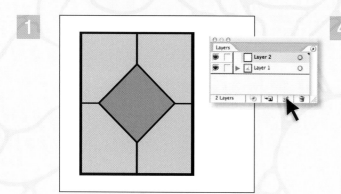

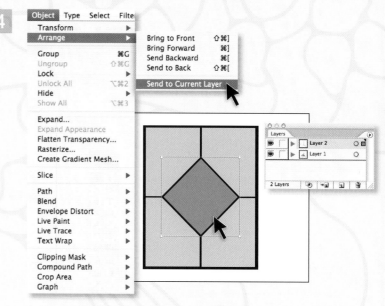

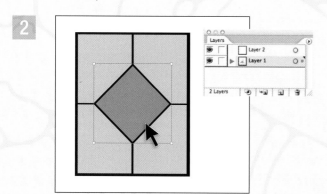

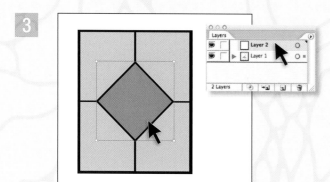

1. On the top menu bar, go to the drop-down menu Window>Layers to open the Layers Window. Create a new layer by clicking the New Layer button located in the lower right corner next to the trashcan.

2. Select the images or shapes you want to move to a new layer using the Selection Tool found at the top left corner of the tool bar [V].

3. With the images still highlighted, reselect the new layer (layer 2) by clicking the radio button next to the layer name.

4. On the top menu bar go to the drop-down menu Object>Arrange>Send to Current Layer. This will send all the shapes selected in step 2 to layer 2.

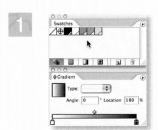

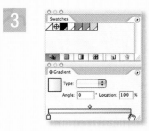

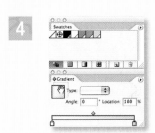

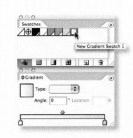

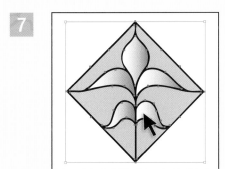

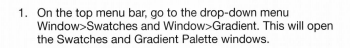

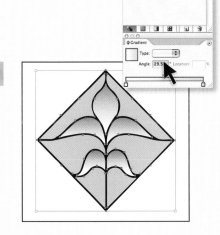

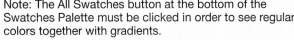

1. On the top menu bar, go to the drop-down menu Window>Swatches and Window>Gradient. This will open the Swatches and Gradient Palette windows.

2. Select the color you want to make into a gradient from the Swatches Palette and hold the left mouse button down while dragging the color swatch to the Gradient Palette window.

3. The swatch is placed on either the left or right hand swatch boxes on the gradient slider. The basic gradient should look similar to figure 3. You can adjust the gradient by moving the sliders and by dragging additional color swatches to the Gradient Palette window.

4. In the upper left hand corner of the Gradient Palette window will be the gradient you have just created. Select it and hold the left mouse button down while dragging it to the Swatches Palette.

   Note: The All Swatches button at the bottom of the Swatches Palette must be clicked in order to see regular colors together with gradients.

5. Your Swatch Palette should look similar to Figure 5.

6. Select the image you want to apply your new gradient to using the Selection Tool found at the top left corner of the tool bar [V].

7. Select your new gradient from the Swatches Palette. Your image should look similar to Figure 7.

8. To change the angle of a gradient, select the object containing the gradient, then type in a new angle in the angle input field in the Gradient Palette Window.

Clipping Masks in Illustrator

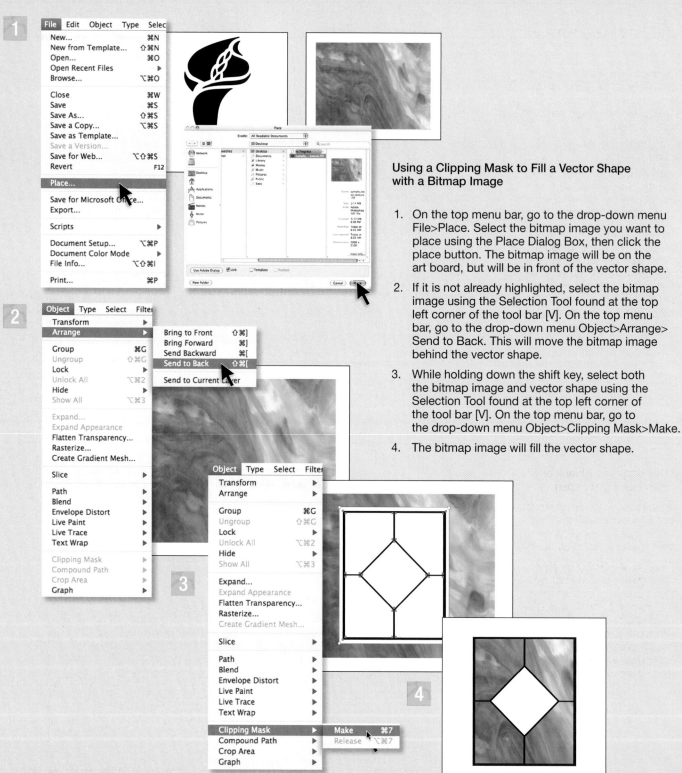

Using a Clipping Mask to Fill a Vector Shape with a Bitmap Image

1. On the top menu bar, go to the drop-down menu File>Place. Select the bitmap image you want to place using the Place Dialog Box, then click the place button. The bitmap image will be on the art board, but will be in front of the vector shape.

2. If it is not already highlighted, select the bitmap image using the Selection Tool found at the top left corner of the tool bar [V]. On the top menu bar, go to the drop-down menu Object>Arrange>Send to Back. This will move the bitmap image behind the vector shape.

3. While holding down the shift key, select both the bitmap image and vector shape using the Selection Tool found at the top left corner of the tool bar [V]. On the top menu bar, go to the drop-down menu Object>Clipping Mask>Make.

4. The bitmap image will fill the vector shape.

Opening a EPS Vector in Photoshop

1. On the top menu bar, go to the drop-down menu File>Open. In the Open Window, find and select the EPS Vector file you want to open and click the Open button.

2. In the Rasterize Generic EPS Format Window, be sure to select a size that is large enough to fill your document. Because you are rasterizing the EPS, you will not be able to scale the image again without losing quality.

   Remember when working with pixel-based formats in Photoshop, it is always easier to scale down than up. Only EPS Vector files allow you to scale your images without loss of quality before embedding them into your Photoshop document. Not all EPS files are true vector-based objects.

Placing a EPS Vector in Photoshop

1. Be sure to have a blank or working document already open.

2. On the top menu bar, go to the drop-down menu File>Place. In the Open Window, find and select the EPS Vector file you want to place and click the Place button.

3. The EPS Vector will be placed in your blank document and will retain many of its vector-based qualities until it is rasterized. In Photoshop, this is called a Smart Object, since you can still edit it in its native format with a program such as Adobe Illustrator. Read more about Smart Objects in your Photoshop Web Help or the manual that accompanied your software.

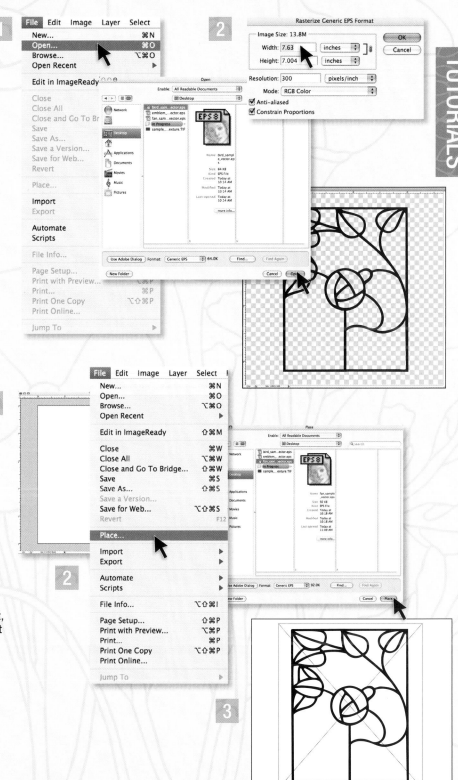

1. Select the Magic Wand Tool [W] found in the tool bar.

2. Enter a value in the Tolerance field found near the top menu bar. The higher this value, the wider the range of colors that will be selected. You can change this value in accordance to the type of image you are using.

3. Select an area of the image.

Adding Color with the Paint Bucket in Photoshop

1. Select the Paint Bucket Tool [G] found in the tool bar.

   The Paint Bucket will use the color assigned to the foreground color box

2. Paint the object by clicking on it.

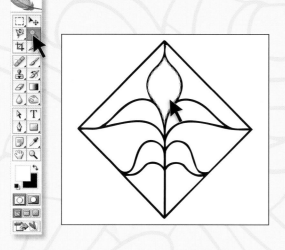

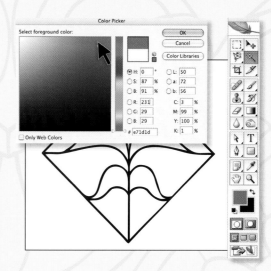

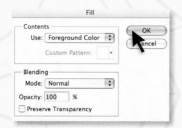

1. Select an area of the image using the Magic Wand Tool [W] found in the tool bar.

2. Double-click the Foreground Color box found at the bottom of the tool bar and open the Color Picker Palette. Select a color and click OK. The new color should display in the Foreground Color box in the tool bar.

3. On the top menu bar, go to the drop-down menu Edit>Fill. Select Foreground Color from the Fill Dialog Box and click OK

4. The section will be filled with the foreground color.

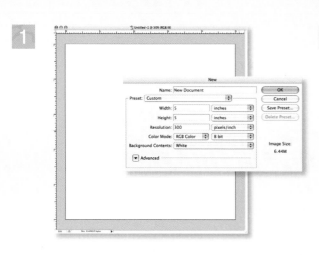

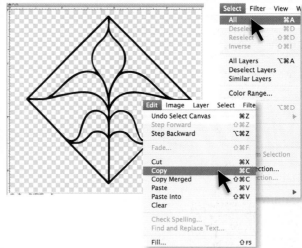

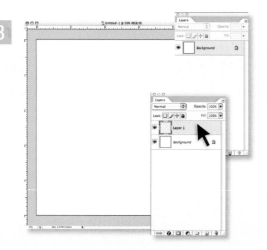

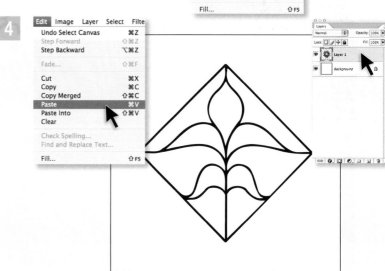

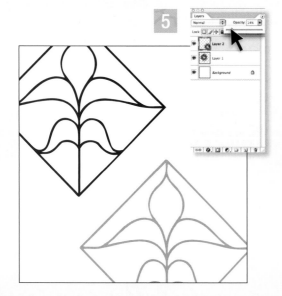

1. On the top menu bar, go to the drop-down menu File>New and create a new blank document.

2. On the top menu bar, go to the drop-down menu File>Open; find and select the EPS Vector file you want in your new document; click the Open button. On the top menu bar, go to the drop-down menu Select>All, then go to the drop-down menu Edit>Copy.

3. Go to the Layers Window in the new blank document made in step 1, and create a new layer by clicking on the New Layer button at the lower right corner next to the trash can.

4. On the top menu bar, go to the drop-down menu Edit>Paste. The vector shape copied in step 2 should now be on Layer 2. Repeat Steps 3 and 4 to add additional layers and images

5   To change the opacity of a layer, select the layer; click the arrow to the right of the Opacity field, and use the slider to manipulate the opacity.

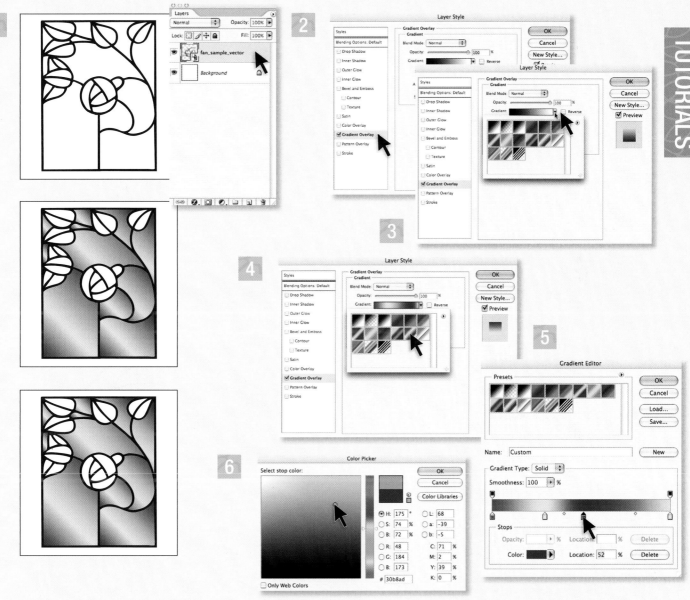

1. In the Layers Window, double-click the layer you want to add a style to. This will open the Layer Style Window.

2. In this window, select Gradient Overlay in the list of styles at the left of the window to open the Gradient Options Window.

3. Click the arrow at the right end of the gradient sample bar.

4. Choose a gradient from the pop-up menu.

5. Click the gradient swatch to open the Gradient Editor Window. Click on any of the color stop boxes to choose new colors.

6. In the Color Picker Window, select a new color and click OK

   You can also change the position of the color stop boxes by sliding them along the gradient bar

1. Open a line art stained glass EPS image from the CD. (see page 41) Then Convert its color space to RBG by going to the top menu bar, drop down menu Image>Mode>RGB

2. Open an image of glass from the CD.

3. Select a cell of the image using the Magic Wand Tool [W] found in the tool bar. (see page 42)

   Be sure to set the tolerance at 32, with both Anti-Alias and Contiguous checked when making your selection.

   Smooth the selection 2 pixels via the top menu bar, drop-down menu Select>Modify>Smooth. Click OK

   Then Expand the selection by 2 pixels by going to the top menu bar, drop-down menu Select>Modify>Expand. Click OK

4. Click on the glass document you want to incorporate into the selected cell.

   On the top menu bar, go to the drop-down menu Select>All. This should select the entire glass image.

   Then from the top menu bar, go to the drop down menuEdit>Copy. This will copy the selection

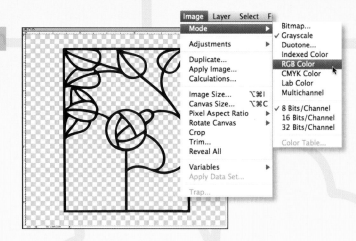

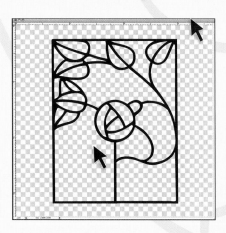

4

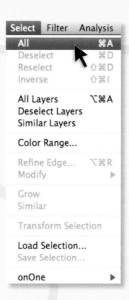

5

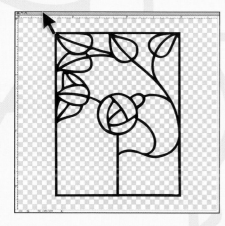

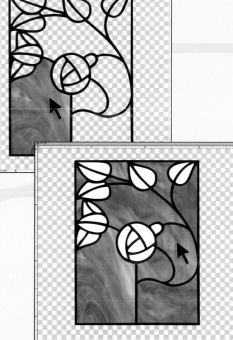

5. Click back on the b/w line art image. Be sure a cell is still selected, if not repeat step 3.

   On the top menu bar, go to the drop-down menu Edit>Paste Into. The copy (step 4) of the glass image should be pasted inside the selected cell.

   Repeat Steps 2 thru 5 to finish filling in the cells of the stain glass line art.

Once the glass images have been pasted into the b/w line art (see pages 46-47), they can then be transformed to better simulate real stained glass.

1. To scale the glass, select an individual pane with the Selection Tool [V] found at the top of the Tool Bar. This should also highlight the Layer the pane is on as well.

2. On the top menu bar, go to the drop-down menu Edit>Transform>Scale.

3. Scale the image using the handles that pop-up around the selection.

    When the image has been scaled to your liking simply double click the left mouse button and the transform will be set.

4. To rotate the glass select an individual pane with the Selection Tool [V] found at the top of the Tool Bar

5. On the top menu bar, go to the drop-down menu Edit>Transform>Rotate.

6. Rotate the image using the handles that pop-up around the selection.

    When the image has been rotated to your liking simply double click the left mouse button and the transform will be set.

The expressive range of the 24 glass samples supplied on the CD can be dramatically expanded by using the Hue and Saturation function in Photoshop.

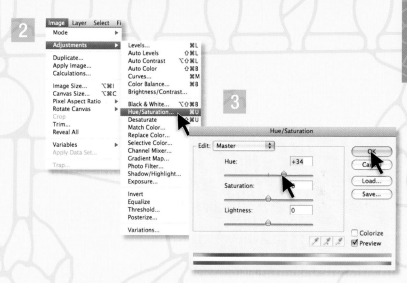

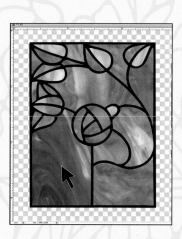
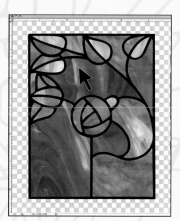
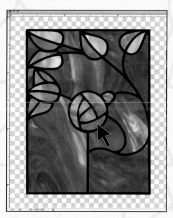

1. To change the color of the glass select an individual pane with the Selection Tool [V] found at the top of the Tool Bar.

2. On the top menu bar, go to the drop-down menu Image>Adjustments>Hue/Saturation.

3. In the Hue/Saturation dialog box simply vary the color using the Hue Slider Bar.

    Once you have the color that you want click the OK button to set the new color.

    Continue this process to create a visually stunning piece of digital stained glass art.

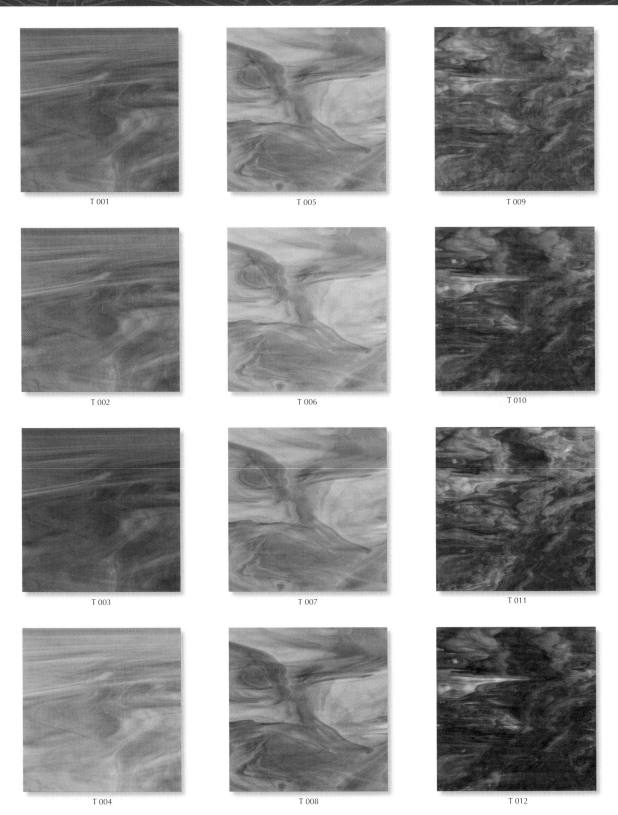

Smoke 1	Smoke 2	Swirl 1
T 001	T 005	T 009
T 002	T 006	T 010
T 003	T 007	T 011
T 004	T 008	T 012

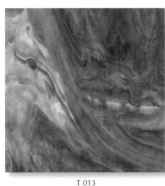

T 013

T 017

T 021

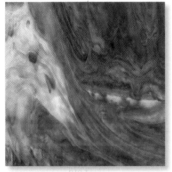

T 014

T 018

T 022

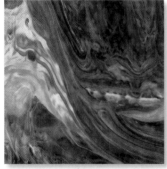

T 015

T 019

T 023

T 016

T 020

T 024

STAINED GLASS TEXTURES

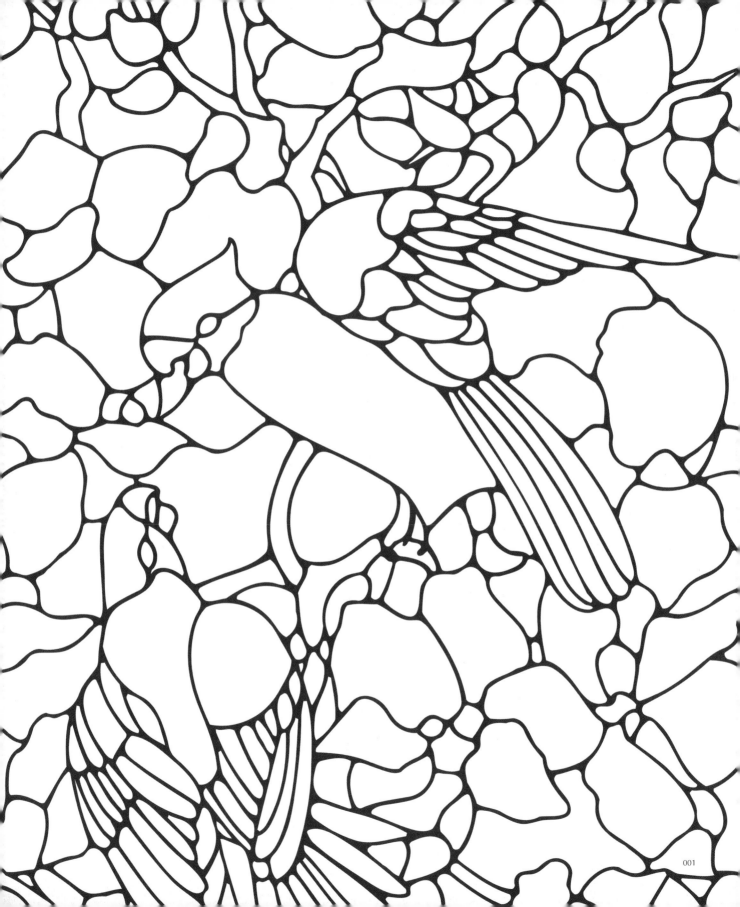

002

003

004

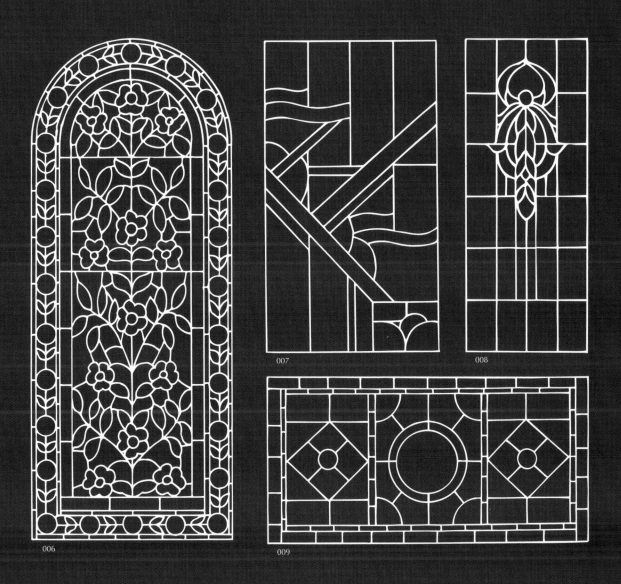

006

007

008

009

010

011

012

013

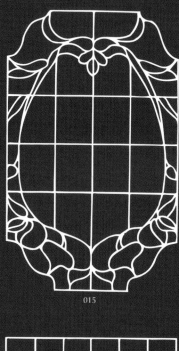

015

016

017

018

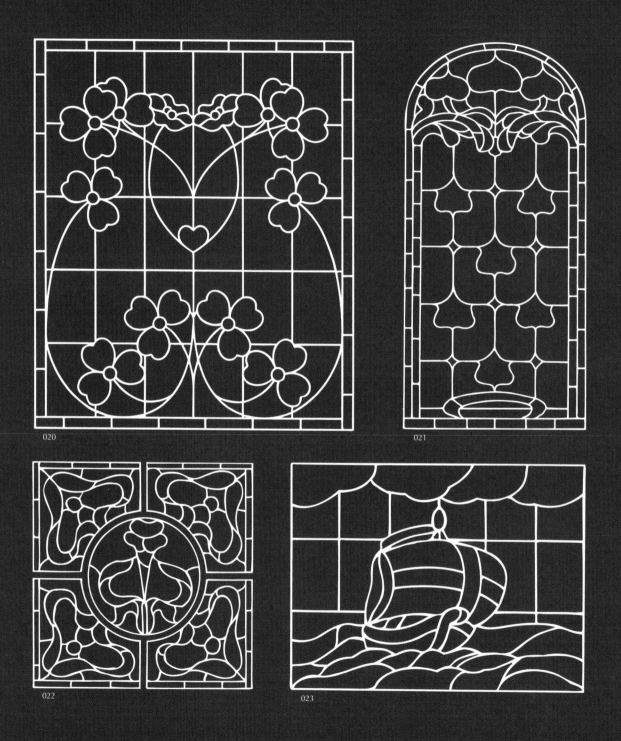

020

021

022

023

024

025

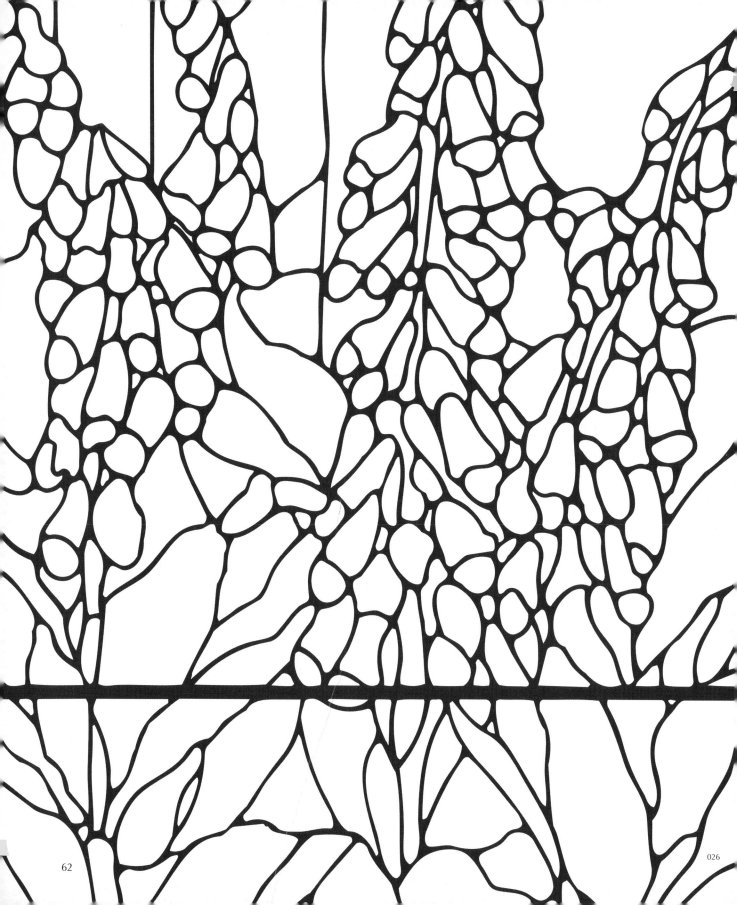

027

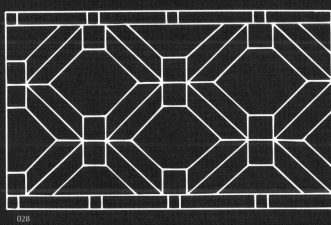

028

029

030

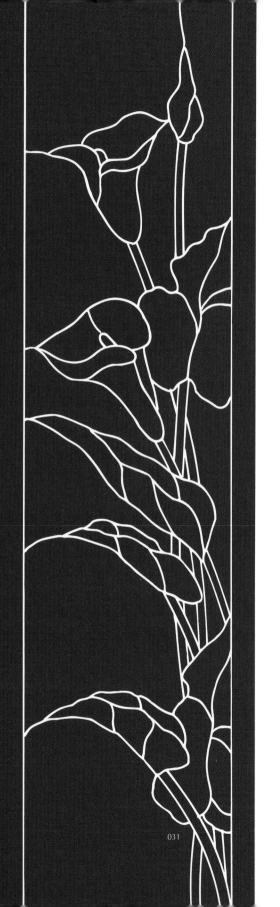

031

032

033

034

035

036

037

038

039

040

041

043

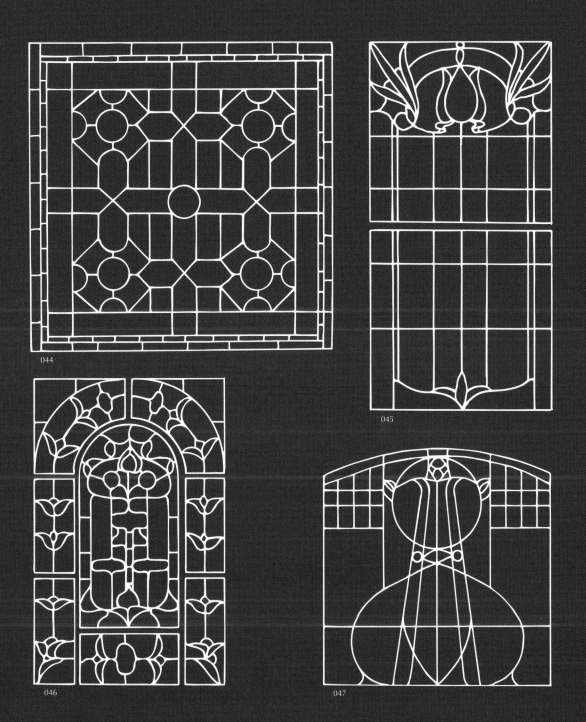

044

045

046

047

048

049

050

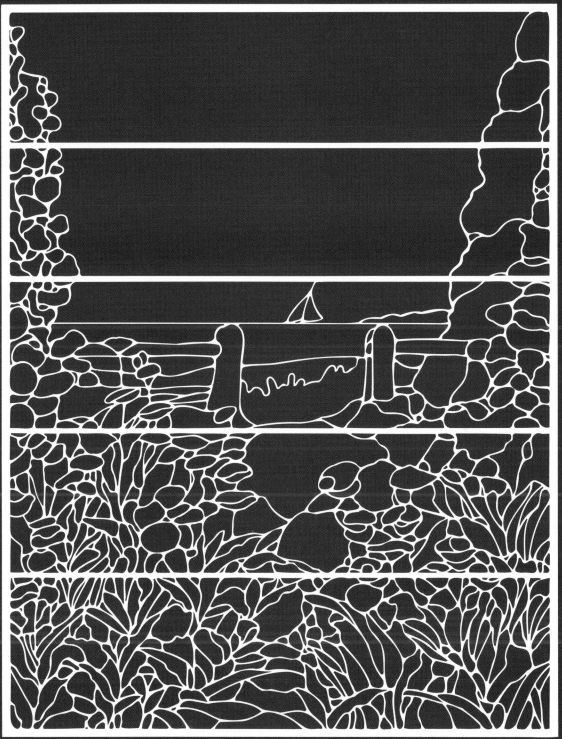

051

052

053

054

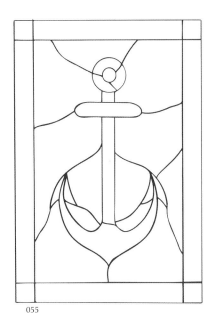

055

056

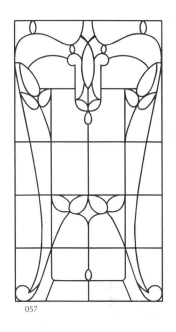

057

058

060

061

062

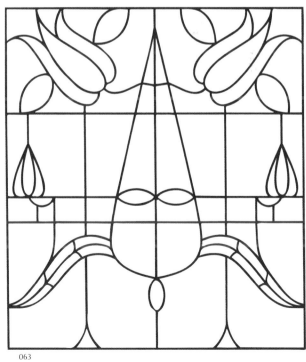

063

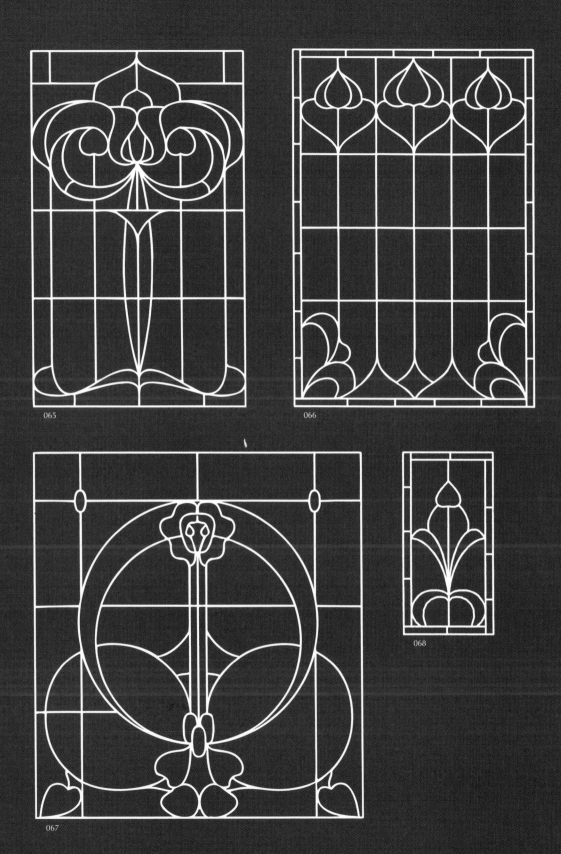

065

066

067

068

069

070

071

072

074

075

076

077

078

079

080

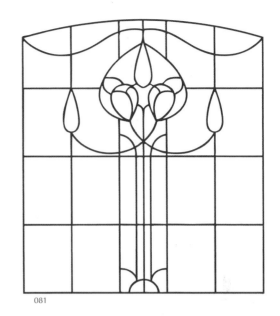

081

082

083

084

085

086

087

088

089

090

091

092

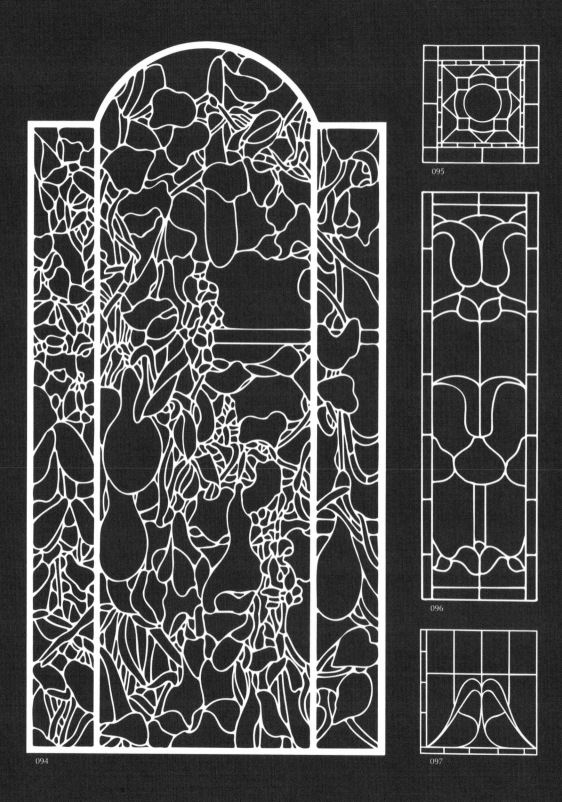

094

095

096

097

100

101

102

103

104

105

106

107

108

109

110

111

112

113

114

115

116

117

118

119

120

121

122

123

124

125

126

127

128

129

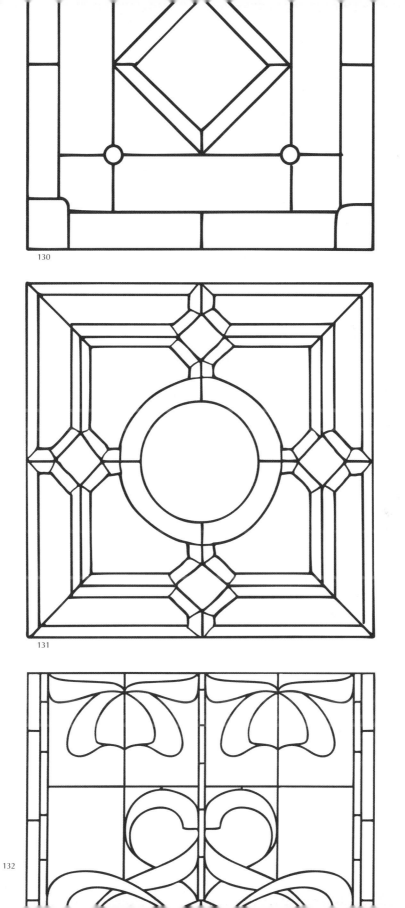

130

131

132

133

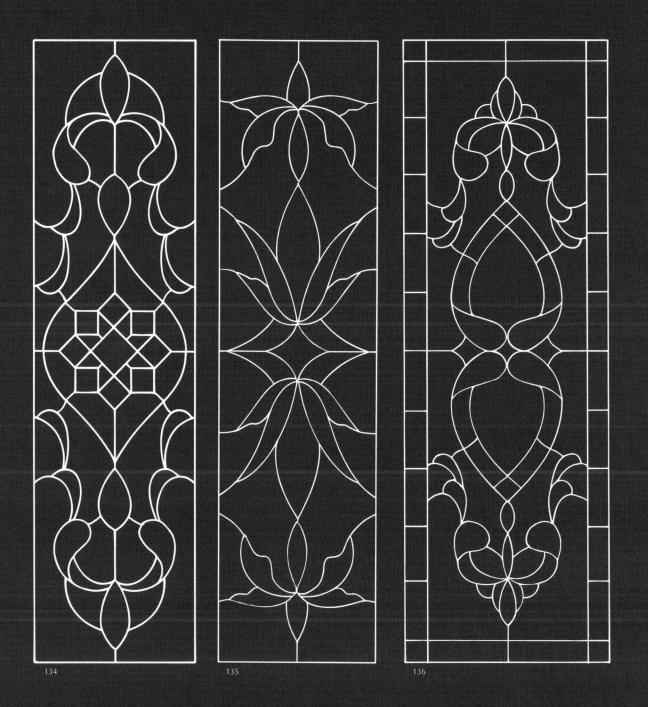

134

135

136

137

138

139

140

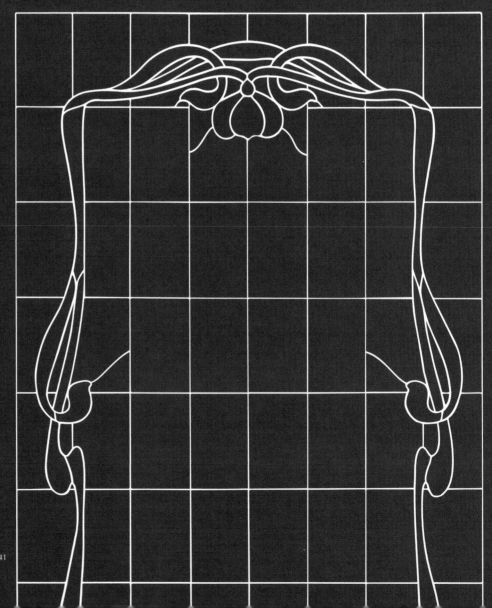

141

142

143

144

145

146

147

148

149

150

151

152

153

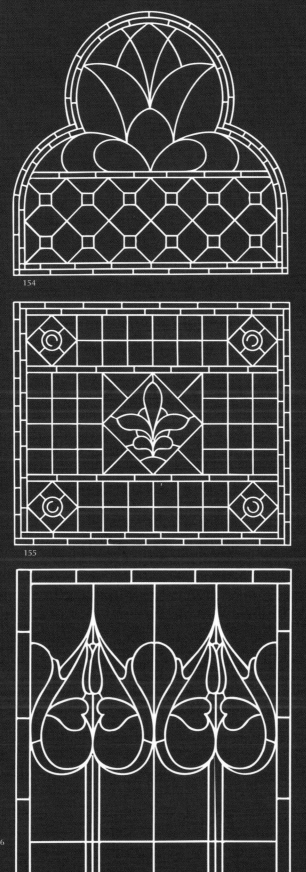

154

155

156

158

159

160

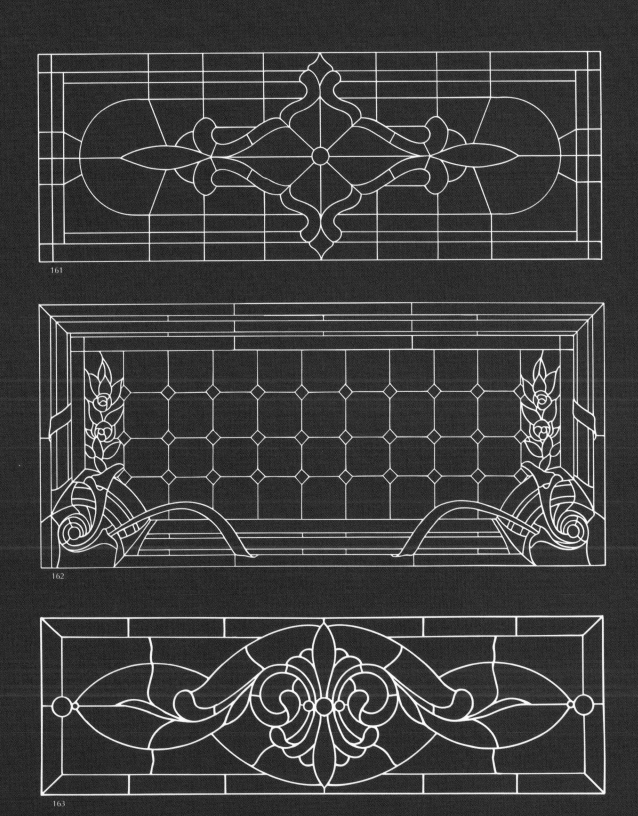

161

162

163

164

165

166

167

168

169

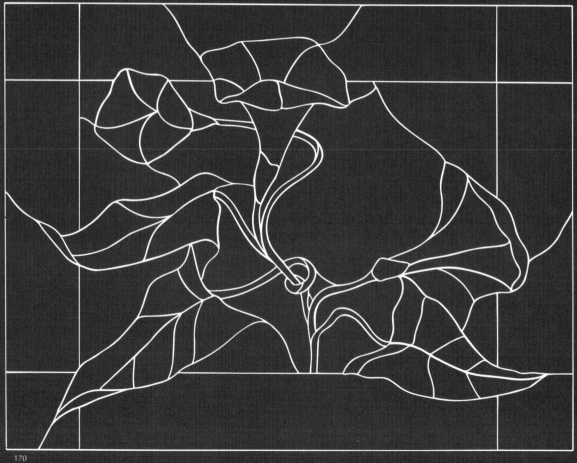

170

171

172

173

117

174

175

176

177

178

179

180

181

182

183

184

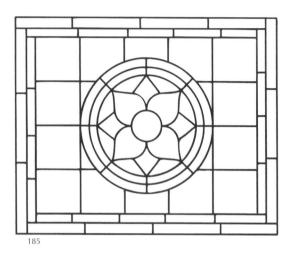

185

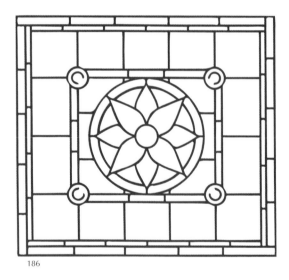

186

187

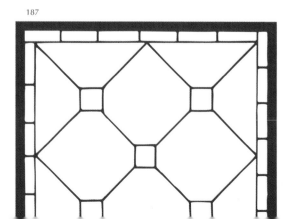

188

189

190

191

124

192

193

195

194

196

197

198

199

200

201

WHAT'S ON THE CD

EPS and SVG vector files of all of the images in the Vectors section.
JPG bit-mapped files of all of the images in the Vectors section.
EPS vector files of all of the vector textures used in the Gallery section.
JPG files of all of the bitmap textures used in the Gallery section.
JPG files of all of the illustrations in the Gallery section of the book.
Dover Design Manager

SOFTWARE AND HARDWARE REQUIREMENTS

The vector images on the included CD are suitable for use on computers running Windows 98, 2000, XP or Vista; or Macintosh OS 9.1–OS X. The computer should have sufficient RAM to power the type of graphics software program with which these image files are intended for use; 256MB minimum, 512MB recommended.

To fully utilize these vector images they must be used with an illustration program such as Adobe Illustrator®, Macromedia Freehand®, or Corel Draw®, or a web animation program such as Adobe Flash®. The images can also be opened, but with limited functionality, in pixel image-editing programs such as Adobe Photoshop®, Adobe Photoshop Elements®, and Corel PaintShop®. This book and CD does not contain any of the above software.

The vector images in this book were based on artwork
taken from the following previously published Dover titles:

Tiffany Windows Stained Glass Pattern Book, by Connie Clough Eaton;
Victorian Stained Glass Designs CD-ROM and Book, by Hywel G. Harris;
Decorative Doorways Stained Glass Patterns CD-ROM and Book, by Carolyn Relei;
Traditional Stained Glass Designs CD-ROM and Book, by Dover;
Traditional and Contemporary Stained Glass Designs CD-ROM and Book, by Joel Wallach.